EXPRESSIONS OF AN EDUCATOR

Insights and Foresights

Errakiah Sannasi

Illustrated by

Celine Soon

INDIA • SINGAPORE • MALAYSIA

ISBN
Paperback 979-8-89519-855-1
Hardcase 979-8-89673-401-7

DEDICATION

Dedicated to

My Parents: Sannasi Errakkiah
Akkammah Narasimalu

My Wife: Jokamalar V. Kumarasamy

&

To all

Promoters of Alternate Energies

addressing Climate Change and

Global Warming

Educators and Students

Lovers of catchy Quotations and Sayings

"Affection and devotion keep a family together"

PREFACE

I kindly invite book lovers to my literary world of around two hundred and fifty expressions conveyed in prose and verses on the lifestyles and challenges of mankind on this magnificent blue planet.

I indeed hope my thoughts, insights, foresights and ideas expressed can be used up as citable quotations and sayings. They can be applied to add colour to speeches and writings, as value added and also to bring home convincing messages.

I request you to spend your invaluable time to peruse and rejoice in these succinct expressions that well crystallize the wisdom of my lifetime experiences in this world. All I ask of you is to explore my world of thoughts and dreams with me.

I believe your exploration into the potential quotations and sayings in this text will be worthy of your investment and time. Welcome to my work and have an enjoyable read.

"God is the Playwright. His Play is Man"

JAN. 2024 Errakiah Sannasi

"Whatever you endeavor to accomplish
do it in style to make a difference in your performance"

CONTENTS

LOVE

Love conquers one and all

To be in love is awe-inspiring

Love is the sweetest of pleasures

True lovers stick together for life

Their hearts beat as one all through

THE MAGIC OF LOVE
(FALLING AND RISING IN LOVE)

Love seems like nothing but means something

It is not just anything but a mutual adoring

binding a couple to a lifelong bonding

⅄

Love at first sight triggers with vibrations

Out of the blue it blooms and blossoms

What charm enthralls the eyes of the beholders!

⅄

Love is not a fleeting feeling but a sustainable passion

It comes alive and lively with positive interaction

and infuses meaning to the relation

⅄

The magic of love defies all logic and reason

and is portrayed as a blind sentimental attraction

Is love a play of hormones or a preordained affection?

⅄

LOVE EVERYWHERE

**Love is reverence to parents, deference to elders,
comradeship to friends, affection towards children,
kindness to domiciled pets, concern for eco-world,
patriotism to the nation and devotion to the Divine**

⅄

**Love is a sentimental mutual affection between lovers.
Its mystical appeal, magical charm, chemistry, affection,
admiration, devotion, excitement, fascination, fondness,
intense passion and romance, overrules and overwhelms**

⅄

PASSION OF LOVE

The power of love has the vigor to rule the world

The passion of love has the fire to rock the world

Power and passion of love dominate the world

⅄

Love overwhelmed by utter passion, romance and lust

drives a pleasure-seeking man wild and crazy

Sensational love bonds lovers pretty intimately

⅄

Intense love finds expression in physical pleasure

Love lasts so long as love lusts

⅄

Falling in love is an illusion

It is self-love disguised as passion for the other

Soon this illusion dissipates and what love remains?

⅄

MEASURE

However much patience the art of love require
All sufferings and tribulations, I'll truly endure
Meet up challenges and confront rivalries I dare
Whenever or wherever I'm sought, I will be there

⅄

Whatever it takes, I will stick to you, I dare swear
All disappointments and troubles I'll bravely bear
Anything and everything adorable I will surely hire
and make you my exclusive wholehearted life partner

⅄

A COMMITMENT

Love is a spell cast by the illusion and obsession
of a woman's beauty and a man's flattery
Once broken they see reality

⅄

A man is intoxicated by a woman's looks
A woman is impressed by a man's compliments
They float in ecstasy till they come out of their fantasy

⅄

Love is neither a bed of roses nor all pleasures
but valleys and hills to ascend and traverse
Challenges in love forge firm steadfast lovers

⅄

Love is not merely clasping of hands, romance
Or a momentary lust but a sustainable passion
and a crucial commitment to the relationship

⅄

WAIT NO LONGER

Wait not my dear till I am gone and no more
Pen your poetry of love and recite it to me now
Hold me tight and whisper your love in my ears
Pass the roses now, and hug me more and more

A WONDERFUL FEEL

Love enables survival and acceptance
regardless of imperfections and tribulations
Time passes, love not only perseveres but also thrives

⅄

Love is caring and respecting, receptive and responsive
It is being comfortable and enlivened in companionship
True love is the heart and soul of a lifelong bond

⅄

Being in love is a spellbinding experience
By all means feel heaven's paradise and hell's fire

⅄

Love is accepting all that was, is and will be
Love lasts as long as love lasts

⅄

MARRIAGE

With a mismatched spouse you'll be weary
With a monotonous spouse you'll be dreary
When completely disillusioned you'll be sorry

With a compatible spouse life will be cheery
Raising a family is demanding yet rewarding

A MARVELOUS CREATION

Woman is a symbol of beauty, embodiment of love,
epitome of motherhood, quintessence of patience,
depiction of tolerance and fountain of compassion.

⅄

The mysterious heart of a woman is
as unfathomable as the ocean and
unpredictable as the weather

⅄

A woman is God's greatest gift to man as
a grandmother, a mother, a wife and daughter
A man is her indispensable sharing partner

⅄

In God's creation the woman is privileged
with the noble function of birthing and nurturing
the posterity of the human species

⅄

BRING TO A CLOSE

A woman typically has the final word
A man ostensibly loses in all the battles
hoping to outwit her in the ensuing war
All's said and done, he loses this war too

⅄

A woman's most enchanting ornament is her smile
and when she is also pretty, smart and persuasive
the man is reduced to a submissive, compliant role
A husband is the king in the family but in name only

⅄

AN EYE OPENER

A woman is all to a man - his dream and his world
She is his love, his heartthrob
and most of all, his life

⅄

A marital life is a blend of pleasurable moments
as well as unanticipated disillusionment
Exorbitant dowries are demanded in some marriages

⅄

Married life is indeed a bitter-sweet experience
It's a paradise yet hell, real yet an illusion

⅄

Infatuated couples who are cupid's casualty
or match-made sadly with no compatibility
soon find their marriage an eye opener in reality

⅄

MAINTAIN THE SPARK

Marriages shake if threatened, worse if betrayed
All issues with exception of betrayal can be solved
if the spark in them is kept alive and ever thriving
Won't sincerity and trust bind two to a lasting bond?

⅄

MARRIAGE TO THE END

A marriage is not merely
a union of just two people but two families
It is a binding intended for lifelong bonding

⅄

Relationships are many in life
but one who travels with you for life
is your better half

⅄

A son married is a son lost
A daughter is always a daughter

⅄

A marriage that evolves into a family
is neither for awhile nor for a trial
but for life

⅄

HAPPINESS

If there's any thing in life much more than
the delight of success and satisfaction
it's the feeling of happiness

Laughter and smiles are exclusive gifts
bestowed upon the human alone

GREATEST JOY

Happiness is not in ecstasy or affluence
It is neither conditional nor consequential
What then is happiness?

⅄

Happiness is an inner feeling of joyfulness
that blooms from within the self

⅄

Be cheerful and delightful in celebrations
A party without laughter and fun is no party at all
Make each other cheery and merry

⅄

Happiness is the ultimate joy of human existence
Happy is he who is mindful and peaceful
with his family and at work

⅄

ENJOY YOUR STAY

Happiness is neither measured by your riches nor by the celebrities you mingle with but by the sparkling faces you generate around you

Plants grow healthy with water and sunshine

Faces glow pretty with happiness and smiles

⅄

The world is full of amazing marvels and wonders

Enjoy your stay with fun and laughter all the way

Fortunate is the human race to live a life on Earth

He who is happy and composed within is capable of contributing to the serenity of the surroundings

⅄

HAPPIERTIMES

Happiness is the basis of energy for all our actions and deeds in the world

One is at his best when he performs with fun and joy

⅄

Companions make events ecstatic and merrier

True friends stick around all times

⅄

Happiness shared is maximized

Sorrow shared is minimized

⅄

Happiness embraces him who is engrossed

with fun and laughter all the way through his life

⅄

LIFESTYLE

Head or tail- game of chance

This or that - a matter of choice

Success or failure -there's a price

Life and time can neither

be retracted nor undone

LIFE IS EXPERIENCE

Birth and Death are doings of the Almighty Divine
The life in-between is your choice of preferences
on what to hold on to and what to let go

⅄

Birth on earth is a call to souls to involve and evolve
by way of life for a destined duration and purpose
Death either liberates life or begins another life for the soul

⅄

Life is a struggle for survival and perseverance
The diligent and resilient brace themselves against
hard times and surprises

⅄

Life isn't just a puzzle to resolve or a crisis to reconcile
It's a wonder to discover, an experience to uncover

⅄

DELIGHT OF LIFE

It is not the number of friends in your life but the type of friends around you that matters

It is not the quantity of years in your life but the quality of life in your years that decides

⅄

Life is already trying and tough

Attempt not to complicate it further and then go around complaining about it

Life on earth is indeed a formidable challenge

⅄

ENJOY YOUR MOMENTS

Life is full of deliberations, decisions and advances
It is a challenge indeed to excel and keep excelling
No man gets all things desired without any effort

⅄

The beauty and joy of art is in the painting
The quality and measure of life is in the living

⅄

Life is not winning all the while or losing all the time
You win sometimes, you lose sometimes
You win some, you lose some

⅄

Lives emerge and perish incessantly
on the face of the earth like ripples and bubbles
that appear and disappear continuously in the waters

⅄

TO YOU, YOUR LIFE

Lessons of life are best learnt in the real world
Some are determinedly riding high to the top
Many are sadly sliding down to the bottom.
Others stand aside gazing and pondering

⅄

Life is real only while you are alive and around
Once you are no more, it matters not anymore
The journey of life finally vanishes into oblivion
Such is the end result of all lives on planet Earth?

⅄

MYSTERY OF LIFE

What is relationship if we are not for each other?
Life is not life if we have not lived a benevolent life
People are naturally better of together

⅄

The greatest suspense in life is the surprise
awaiting to shock us at any moment

Life seems real while breathing and kicking.
It turns an illusion when packing and leaving

⅄

We arrive with nothing, strive for everything,
live with something, leave without anything.

⅄

LIFE IS AN ILLUSION

Life is a delusion that takes you
On a life-long pursuit of a mirage
Only when you stop, you realize that
You've been actually chasing a fantasy

DRAMA IN A DREAM

Life is meaningful when there is freedom
to explore and experiment your aspirations
Create a haven around you and press forward

⅄

Love is a burden when there is no trust
Life is a burden when there is no peace
Religion is a burden when there is no faith

⅄

All fascination, glamour and charm in life
are merely momentary fantasies

⅄

Life is an unparalleled gift to man
Is he making the most and the best of it?

⅄

EDUCATION

Before a successful nation, there's a leader
Behind a successful spouse, there's a partner
Beside a successful student, there's a teacher

Man is a lifelong learner
The world is an eternal teacher

KNOWLEDGE FOR LIVING

Exploring and discovering is lifetime learning
Life is educating and enlightening people constantly
It's neither too old nor too late to pursue learning

⅄

Beside every trainee there is an instructor
Behind every entrepreneur there is a mentor
After every professional there is a professor

⅄

All that we picked up from the cradle onwards
will follow through to our last breath in this world

⅄

Educational institutions primarily equip students with
knowledge, values and skills to live a commendable life

⅄

GOAL OF EDUCATION

The main object of education is inculcation
of values, promotion of a civilized quality life,
development of serenity within one's own self
and inducing harmony with the natural world

INSPIRING TEACHERS

**Behind and beside every student is a teacher
who imparts a world of knowledge and values
Caring parents follow up closely with teachers
to monitor the performance of their children**

TEACHERS

A dedicated and diligent teacher pushes prods even jabs to lift students to the next phase

He essentially prepares them to handle their future

⅄

A born teacher is an artist

and his medium is an evolving tool

⅄

As a teacher it is crucial, not to give up on a student

A conscientious teacher treats all students alike

Students should be free to articulate and express

⅄

A teacher is not an encyclopedia on the stage

but a guidebook by the side

⅄

KNOWING REAL SELF

Education isn't just a process of enhancing lifestyle
or developing the ingenuity to innovate and invent
but a means to comprehend and knowing oneself
It's the basis of knowledge, information and wisdom

⅄

Absence of quality education retards mankind
Inadequacy in education will cripple the nation
Educate the mother, the family becomes educated
Educate the population, the nation moves forward

⅄

I'M THE SUNSHINE

I'm the light that dispels darkness around you

I'm the sight that opens up the world to you

I'm the map that guides you all along the way

⅄

I don't wear out, however much utilized

The more I'm used, the more I top you up

⅄

When I'm embraced and utilized, you will live

If I'm ignored and shunned, you will merely exist

⅄

The illiterate and naive differ from the learned and elite

as the blind differ from the sighted

⅄

WINNER

Regret not the past, yesterday was experience

Fret not the future, tomorrow will be suspense

Waste not the present, today is performance

Only the champion is remembered

All other contestants are forgotten

A DREAM

A dream remains a fantasy till it becomes a reality
The realization of a vision necessitates a mission
And the life-wire of a mission is absolute passion

⅄

Go-getters would embark on new horizons
rather than trudge on worn out paths of prospects

⅄

Challenges introduce a man to himself
No fighter becomes a champ
until he rises-up to fight

⅄

It's not only what you know but also whom you know
that takes you to the threshold of opportunities

⅄

MOVE ON FOR MORE

A loser crumbles and relinquishes in crisis

A winner strives and thrives in trying times

A loser aborts and retreats in severe stress

A winner persists and battles till he attains

⅄

The mere taste of triumph, applause and ovation can blow up your modest mind and puff your chest

Let not all your splendid winnings swell your head

Get prepared and move on to the next race on time

⅄

A WINNER

Small minds are short sighted and hind sighted

Great minds are farsighted and foresighted

A sane mind in a sound body is a brilliant blend

⅄

Failure is the consequence of apathy and indolence

Victory surfaces with ingenuity and diligence

⅄

Get your winter coat well before the season

Winter is coming sooner or later for certain

⅄

One's strife and strike should be timely

to hit the target precisely

⅄

CLARITY IN ACTION

Keep your vision and mission in the forefront,

all challengers and competitors at a distance,

setbacks, letdowns, washouts and flops behind

but the family beside to attain greater heights

WINNERS PERSIST

Winning comes not easy

but with mistakes and failures

No learning takes place without faults and errors

⅄

Never expect total perfection in human deeds

Errors and blunders are learning opportunities

⅄

Most of all

Do what you love and love what you do

Winning will follow

⅄

It's not so much, how often you win in life

but winning life itself, that matters most in life

⅄

WORK CONSISTENTLY

Step after step and all the time on it propels a dancer to utmost excellence

Word by word closely attending to it transforms a script into a masterpiece

MAKE THE DIFFERENCE

It's not merely being the most diligent or resilient

but surfacing as the most responsive to changes that keeps one going.

⅄

Mistakes are friends

Every winner crosses his failures and

embraces success eventually.

⅄

Winning comes with strategy

sacrifice and relentless effort all the way

⅄

Exist not merely as another person in this world.

Conduct your life as a role model to others.

⅄

ADVERSITY

In the history of humanity
there is no better lesson than adversity
Hard times fortify the will to persevere

Who manages adversities
survives in critical crisis

PRINCIPLES AND AVARICE

Inducements penetrate all nooks and crannies

as avariciousness and temptation grip both the

beneficiaries and benefactors for mutual benefits

⅄

The way to come out a winner in a gambling den

is by crushing the inclination to betting altogether

No amount of remorse can redress gaming losses

⅄

Adversities conversely reinforce the resilience in man

to withstand calamities, disasters and misfortunes

⅄

The avaricious and dishonest who succumb to wrong doings

ultimately bear the consequences of greed and fraudulence

⅄

NATURAL CALAMITIES

Natural world is crucial for the survival of all species
The eco system maintains the inter-relationship between
the living organisms and the environment
Man has to live in harmony with the natural world

⅄

With no more greens and grains, trees and fruits,
cattle and fowls, rivers and fishes, flora and fauna,
provisions and groceries, pure water and clean air, and
suitable food stuff, our life is indeed sacrificed

⅄

NATURAL DISASTER

It is absolutely pertinent to address climate change and
global warming and regulate bio-engineering expansions
to preserve lives and the Mother Earth

⅄

Natural disasters are turning into global crisis
A clean energy revolution is crucial to combat
the climate catastrophe and global warming

⅄

Little does man realize the nature he devastates
is the very creation of the Almighty Divine he reveres

⅄

Man battling fellow man defeats or ends up defeated
Man at war with nature is himself the ultimate casualty

⅄

HISTORY REPEATS

After a nuclear world war, nations will still battle but with clubs, bows and arrows till history repeats itself

Neither the League of Nations nor the United Nations succeeded in civilizing man despite the two world wars

DESTRUCTION FOR RICHES

Man leaves trails of destruction in pursuit of constructions and development

Why does man blind himself for transient riches?

⅄

Drug trafficking is becoming a lucrative trade

victimizing the youth and adults all round

⅄

The virulent diseases presently prevalent

in the world are taking a toll on human lives

⅄

It takes one lunatic, narcissistic tyrant

to explode a nuclear bomb that can flatten the earth

and wipe out lives instantaneously

⅄

A SAFE LIFE

A world free of pollution, viruses and nuclear missiles are
today's top priorities for a healthier and safer life

The world needs to check on the unscrupulous leaders

who are not mindful of security of humankind on Earth

NURTURE NATURE

Climate catastrophe resulting in flash floods and
global warming is testimony to nature provoked

⅄

Love and care for Mother Earth
as you would love and care your own mother

⅄

Nature secures the evolution
and survival of life on this Blue Planet

⅄

Go green, nurture nature and liven up
the planet Earth

⅄

BALANCING

Balancing lifestyles is an art
Matching and balancing disputes
harmonize conflicting relationships

However thin a piece is carved
there will always be two sides to it

EMERGE AND SUBSIDE

From start to finish, life is ups and downs,
rising and subsiding like the waves in the seas
Happiness and sorrow are part and parcel of life

⅄

Human life is neither all perfect nor all flawed
Good and bad tag along from womb to tomb

⅄

Being forthright and reserved, strict and lenient
are some of the inherent traits in humankind
Matching disagreements is a sensible balance

⅄

A balanced person is optimistic as well as pessimistic,
sometimes positive and at times negative

⅄

BALANCE THE EXTREMES

Life is a formidable balance between extremes

It's sometimes real and at times rather illusive

Levelheadedness in mankind is the pre requisite for matching and balancing extreme situations

⅄

BALANCING IS INDISPENSABLE

The waxing and waning of the monthly moon, the days and nights in the daily routine are Natures balances

The balance between male and female genders of lives ensures their continuous survival on this planet Earth

⅄

GEOPOLITICAL BALANCE

The global Superpowers have endangered mankind
with their creations of sophisticated nuclear missiles
World peace warrants a geopolitical balance of power

⅄

In the domain of political philosophy
socialism is seen as the balance between
communism and democracy

⅄

Human beings are endowed with
the faculty and aptitude to weigh the pros and cons
of situations they find themselves in

⅄

Extremes in worldly ways have to be judiciously
balanced to establish and manage a stable living

⅄

DEBTORS

In monetary dealings a man is either
a financial victor as a smart lender or
a financial victim as a miserable borrower

Years of fret, guilt and regret
can't settle a single cent of debt

TRAUMA OF DEBT

He runs into loans who spends beyond his earnings
There is no need for water, air and sunshine
for debts to grow interest

⅄

A loan from a bank, accrued interest you rightly pay
A loan from a friend, you lose his interest all the way

⅄

When you're in severe debts and tribulations
your kith and kin, dearest and closest
will never hesitate to distant themselves

⅄

An outstanding loan becomes a tormenting debt
An overwhelming debt more often culminates
in an insolvent debtor and an unforgiving lender

⅄

LOSS OF SELF-WORTH

Exorbitant lifestyles, luxuries beyond earnings
and intensifying loans become severe liabilities.
Installment payments form the biggest turn over
for banks but are tormenting burden to borrowers

⅄

A man in debt loses his dignity and self-worth
Trauma of rising debts causes incessant misery
Being in debt is greater tribulation than death
In debts' grips, a debtor dies a thousand deaths

⅄

UNENDING BURDEN

Escalating interests on installment payments
of unsettled debts and loans remain
as unending burden to debtors

⅄

Floundering in debts and threats is a lot more
torturous than living in dire penury and misery

⅄

He loses his poise and peace
who struggles with debts and dues

⅄

Save when you are stable and durable to meet
payments and dues when you are fragile and feeble

⅄

THE WEALTHY

The root of financial evils
is neither money nor ambition
but cupidity and temptation

Money talks, man listens
Riches speak louder than words

POWER OF WEALTH

Promises and pledges are but mere words
Money moves dealings and businesses
It's also money that puts food on the table

⅄

Rules and systems aptly and readily bend
to the affluent and dominant

⅄

The most convenient conduct in life
is in splashing the cash in the wallet

⅄

When it's money, modern man turns crazy
He spends his entire life chasing after money

⅄

LUXURIES TO POVERTY

Man has become a slave to luxuries and comforts
The meager underprivileged struggles and survives
The middle class copes with mere basic necessities
The affluent floating in lofty lifestyle calls the shots

MONEY TALKS

Comedians are funny and witty
The world is spinning around the penny
Money begets money

⅄

Money, money everywhere
Here it comes, there it goes

⅄

Ready cash works great wonders
It readily fulfills deals and agreements

⅄

Currency is the measure of value
and the most convenient tool of transaction

⅄

THE NEEDY

Poverty is no shame or a sin
but to remain in it is inexcusable
Poor man's pleas often go unheard

You can't come out of poverty
if you lie still on your back all the time

DOWN- TRODDEN POOR

The poor yearn for the money they can't get hold of
The rich brood over the money they can't keep tight
Money changes hands extensively in circulation

⅄

When you're wealthy, you're the lion king
When you're penniless you're a pond duck

⅄

When dues and liabilities go sky-high
dearest and closest instantaneously fly

⅄

A silver lining in the cloud is the rainbow of hope
to the down trodden poor who are unable to cope

⅄

POVERTY AND PENURY

Poverty is sleeping on bare floor, walking shoeless,
cooking without oil, showering without shampoo,
surviving with minimum groceries and provisions
A pathetic state indeed but it's no excuse to remain

⅄

Being in poverty is as miserable as being in debts
It is very much easier for the affluent to sympathize
with the poor than to get them out of their poverty
Blessed are the souls that do not suffer in dire penury

⅄

LIVING IS SHARING

While some rejoice in caring and sharing

Others are busy amassing and storing

He exists who stashes, he lives who shares

⅄

With lots of money you lose your sleep

With less money you lose your peace

Either way you are the inevitable loser

⅄

The poor are the neglected species on Earth

They have limited concerned relations and friends

⅄

He is blessed whose hands reach out to ease

the lives of the ill-fated poor

⅄

HUMANITY

Men with high intellect, articulate speech
and upright stance are outstanding beings
Are all such people living a commendable life?

Search not in life for an ideal person
Not a soul on Earth is a perfect human

MARVELOUS MAN

All episodes, species and lives on the face of this Earth
are fundamentally ordained by the Divine for reason best
known to His Holiness alone

⅄

Every man is a walking quotation, enriched
with lessons derived from past experiences
But with all these, has he changed for the better?

⅄

Humankind in the present times is in sheer
agony and misery, degrading to a deplorable level
In today's world, a forthright man is indeed a miracle

⅄

Man's intellect and ingenuity, insight and foresight
combined with his wisdom portray him as a distinct species
But his own dire desires turn him into an unscrupulous being

⅄

WAYS OF HUMANKIND

It is typical of man to conflict with himself
with others and the voiceless natural world
Conflict without, man wrestles to his utmost
Conflict within, he feigns to be a philosopher

⅄

Pessimists always whine about difficult times
Optimists are forever hopeful for better times
Idealists usually envision unlikely probabilities
Realists are practical, down-to-earth pragmatists

⅄

TRAITS TO MAINTAIN

Without initiative you are a burden to yourself

Without self-reliance you are a burden to others

Without involvement you are a burden to the world

⅄

In human relations there are neither perpetual allies

nor eternal foes but only incessant interests

⅄

Variety enlivens the ways of mankind

Imagine a world of people same and similar!

⅄

You are you and I am me

Sometimes we are alike, at times different

We're better off learning to live with differences

⅄

BLESSED SPECIES

Man alone bestowed with intellect and wisdom
gifted with feelings of affection and compassion
endowed with smile, laughter, joy and happiness
is the most talented species on our Mother Earth

⅄

Ethics and values fortify the character in humanity
Discipline and attitude determine stability in life
Good conduct and modesty of the yesteryears are
fast eroding traits that are now slipping into oblivion

⅄

SPICES OF LIFE

Every human being is a student and a teacher

Every episode is an experience and a lesson

A commendable life is in a meaningful living

⅄

There is no absolute perfection in humanity

Vices and virtues are the nature of humankind

⅄

Where is humankind heading

in today's crazy world of turmoil and chaos?

⅄

We need leaders who are not in love with themselves

but with fellow humanity

⅄

DESTINY

Providence creates events and shifts one's destiny in unexpected directions for reasons best known to the Heavens

It happens in a split second that happens not in a lifetime

PROGRAMMED DESTINY

Why are we involved in this planet Earth?
Is it our asking and ardent wish to be here
or is it to fulfill someone's dream or drama!

⅄

We are but mundane transient puppets
in the clasp of corporeal mortal bondage

⅄

What's destined for us never avoids us
What evades us was never meant for us

⅄

The Divine keeps record of our deeds and ensures
we rise and fall by our own standards and doings

⅄

STRATEGY AND SUCCESS

We aspire and strategize to attain all that we yearn and crave for in this viable world

Our ultimate achievement and contentment are dependent on our intentions and actions

TRUTH PREVAILS

Right never wrongs, wrong never holds

Divinity ensures no man scores bliss from crime

He loses his soul who is indifferent to wrongdoings

⅄

They who condemn vices but perpetually do wrong

unequivocally live in sin and shame lifelong

⅄

It is gallant to perish fighting wrong and injustice

than to exist compromising principles and values

⅄

They who are morally supportive of prevailing wrongdoings

are also liable to bear the penalty accorded to the offenders

⅄

DIVINE LAW

Are forces of ordained destinies conducting us
or do we work out our own destiny in our life?
Is it a question of aspiring to live a life we desire
or living an ordained life based on that we deserve?

TRUTH WILL SURFACE

You are a thief only when you are caught

Until then you can masquerade as an Angel

In time, truth will come to light to impeach you

⅄

Always stand by the virtuous and the righteous

The wicked flourish only until the truth surfaces

⅄

What is destined cannot be impeded

What's rightfully pronounced should not be retracted

⅄

Seek no escape from the corridors of cause and effect

What goes around certainly comes around

similar to the boomerang and echo

⅄

DEPART CONFUSED

Born ignorant and raised in a complex world
Egg or hen, seed or tree, your God or my God
your religion, my religion, till now unresolved
Man lives baffled and leaves rather perplexed

DEEDS AND DESTINY

There can be no escape from

that which rightfully afflicts and disasters

We will for sure reap what we sow

⅄

I rather be dead and gone

than succumb to criminal carrots

⅄

Is our destiny totally in our hands

or preordained by the heavens?

⅄

Isn't a man's life determined by his desires,

decisions, deeds and the consequential destiny?

⅄

DEPARTURE

We heed not the harbinger of death
while we are still breathing and kicking
When it strikes us, we are no more

Hang on and wait
Today me, tomorrow you

MATTER OF TIME

Death is part and parcel of life that occurs anytime

from day one, we emerge in this world

⅄

Death is an irrefutable, inescapable certainty,

though man attempts to delay its inevitability

It comes any moment it chooses

⅄

Riches and loved ones we leave behind and sigh

No belonging of ours follows us to our grave

⅄

Why tire ourselves out in this temporary station?

After all the toil and hustle we are but just passers-by

⅄

FINAL DAYS OF THE OLD

Imagine a world full of dependent aged people!
They are normally taken for granted but when
they have gone for good, they are deeply missed
Stay together while they are breathing and kicking

⅄

Death is a blessing to the old as a savior from acute illness
and pathetic dependency on the loved ones.
When you are aged, aimless, unhealthy and lonely
death does you a favour to put you in eternal peace

⅄

INDISPENSABLE DEATH

Death is a destined reality striking lives anytime,
anywhere - on the land, in the waters, in the sky
It awaits mankind at prisons, hospitals, homes etc

⅄

Death is neither negotiable nor deferred forever
It comes sooner or later, regardless of you or me
Maybe today, maybe tomorrow certain indeed

⅄

When the man of the house is gone for good
life on earth goes on as usual for most people
but it's no longer the same to his living spouse

⅄

Man dreads death that creeps up on him unwaveringly
No amount of tears or prayers can awaken the dead

⅄

WHEN TIME IS UP

The moment life starts the countdown also begins
You may yearn to stay a little longer to fulfill
your remaining aspirations but when your time comes up
death does not wait for you to settle all your wants

⅄

Death to lives is indispensable at some point of time
No man calls himself happy the whole of his mortal life
Some faiths propagate - death ends one life and begins another
to fulfill the karma over unsettled issues of the past life.

⅄

ALL WILL END

Nothing in this world is certain as birth and death

Arrival and departure are with the Divine

Living our life is in our hands

⅄

There is no medicine, cure or remedy for death

Man till today has not surpassed death

Accept the reality and move on

⅄

Everything has an end in this world

The human race is no exception

Why on earth then, fear and fret death?

⅄

Who called me to this world?

My time here is up, who shall I call now?

⅄

AFTER LIFE

Does death transform us to lingering Ghosts here?
Reincarnate us for another role in the world drama
Place us in heaven or hell as fixed on Judgment Day
Or surrender our soul to the Almighty God's abode?

WHO CAN BEAT DEATH

Birth begins with Questions

Life drifts on searching for Answers

Death comes eventually as the Solution

⅄

It's a matter of time

Be prepared and ready to depart for good

⅄

The only place where all human beings

are equal without problems is the Grave.

⅄

Is man endowed with

his superb intelligence and intellect

able to surmount death?

⅄

DIVINITY

Religions fundamentally point to one God
They merely differ in their approaches of
interpreting, worshiping and serving HIM

Religions for followers
God for us all

UNITY IN DIVINITY

Tolerance is overrated

It is open-mindedness and mutual respect

that nurture inter religious harmony

⅄

Religion is divine when it unifies

It is no more divine when it divides

⅄

Inter religious understanding is the paramount

priority for solidarity and harmony in humanity

⅄

God has a hand in every twist and turn in our life

for reasons best known to HIM

⅄

SPIRITUAL GOODWILL

Christianity, Islam, Hinduism, Buddhism, Sikhism,
Bahaism, Judaism, Taoism, shintoism and others
This religion or that, yours, his, mine, theirs, ours
Of which religion is the Almighty Supreme God?

⅄

Disputes between religious fanatics occur
more often than the debates with atheists and agnostics
Religions ought to be bridges of spiritual goodwill
and not walls of controversy or unending disputes

⅄

PRAYER AND MEDITATION

Prayer takes us to God

Meditation brings God to us

The Almighty Supreme God is our all

⅄

Love brings man and woman together

Prayer brings God and the human together

⅄

Detach attachment, know your real self

and seek spiritual enlightenment

⅄

Body to soul is a burden when there's no renunciation

Soul to itself a burden when there's no enlightenment

⅄

WHY US IN THIS UNIVERSE

Whence and why this universe, the species,
the flora and fauna on the face of the earth,
where man is unique among all the creatures
Are creations for the recreation of the creator?
Wherefore is the Divine's Hand in this creation?

A CHALLENGE TO RELIGIONS

Religious proponents are contending
to convert the human race to their respective faiths
Is this a spiritual or a political-commercial exercise?

⅄

Despite the escalating activities of religions
atheists and agnostics are on the rise

⅄

Assist the poor and the unfortunate
God will bestow HIS blessings upon the benefactor

⅄

People are for themselves
God is for all lives

⅄

WISDOM OF THE DIVINE

What went well for us was sanctioned by the Divine

What did not turn out well, is an obstruction by God to safeguard us from negative consequences ahead

The ending reveals the wisdom of the benign Divine

TO DIVINE FOR SALVATION

When all things cease to function
people turn to the Divine for solution
HE is the ultimate salvation

⅄

Man slips and bungles
The Almighty God fixes and saves

⅄

When the prayer is answered
God is conveniently forgotten
Such is the nature of some human beings

⅄

The Almighty God is the One and Only source
of all that was, that is and that will be
God is one and the same to all

⅄

THE FUTURE

Digitalization, computerization, bio-engineering, multi-media communications, nuclear innovations and outer space explorations - focus of future world

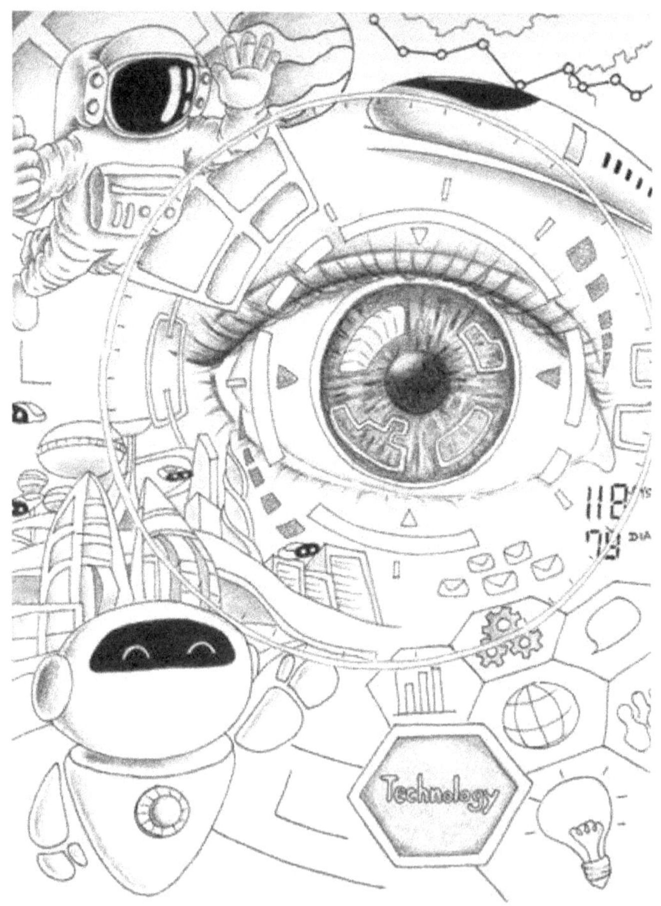

It is possible to speculate generally but rather impossible to predict precisely

APATHY

The despicable, dodgy leaders will continue
riding on the wretched, docile masses
The unfortunate remain in destitute conditions

⅄

Technology will be developing into a gigantic force swallowing
existing principles, values, morals and norms
He loses his soul who is indifferent to wrongdoings

⅄

Conflicts over drinking water, territorial claims,
economic supremacy and religious clashes
are the imminent ongoing issues in global crisis

⅄

Mass migration effected by disasters, conflicts and clashes
escalate the numbers of asylum seekers round the globe

⅄

TECHNOLOGICAL REVOLUTION

In the future years, artificial intelligence and automation play a vital role in digitalization

Learners access a world of knowledge online by the blink of an eye via Contact Lenses

⅄

SAFEGUARD THE EARTH

Environmental pollution, green house gases, carbon monoxide, the melting of snow, rising of the sea levels, flash floods, heat waves and depletion of the ozone layer are the immediate global concerns

⅄

DOOMSDAY

Children are ruthlessly shot down in schools

and the public are gunned down on the streets

Is the gun culture protecting or eliminating lives?

⅄

Nations are piling up nuclear ammunitions as a show

of strength to cope up with fellow nuclear powers

⅄

Diseases are presently taking on the role

of the world wars in wiping out the global populace

⅄

Hey Man!

Aren't your unscrupulous desires and insatiable avarice

drawing you close to your doomsday!

⅄

FINALE

The survival of mankind on this planet can be assured only by a coherent pact between humanity and the natural world

Are men in this world for 'action' Why do they need this experience?

GATEWAYS

Birth and Death are gateways under Divine control

Where and when you emerge and depart is absolutely the prerogative of the holy Divine

⅄

Once you are here the choice is in your hands

to create either a paradise or hell on Earth

The life you live is of your picking and choosing

⅄

Where there is affection there is love

Where there is love, there is life

⅄

Ultimately it's not the assets you gathered

but the life you lived that matters

⅄

LIFE ON EARTH

Man being the smartest of species should be watchful
not to squander away his life for any reason or motive
A commendable life is obviously in a meaningful living
Fortunate are the species living on this Earth of wonders

⅄

ENTRY AND EXIT

Can we capture fleeting time?

Even before we come to grips to half understand life

our entire life comes to an end

⅄

Life is so very short-lived

Chase the life you envisage and enjoy the life you live

⅄

Naked we appeared, crying our eyes out at arrival

Empty we depart, saddened and tearful in farewell

⅄

You can't come out of your life alive but can

make your entry an asset, your exit a loss to the world

⅄

AMAZING

The World is a wonder of wonders in the Universe
Human race is a miracle of miracles among lives
Death is the inevitable mystery of mysteries in life
The holy Divine is the fundamental source of sources

WORLD DRAMA

Who am I in this body and soul
What's my bond with the Divine and the world drama
Is it my ardent wish to be here?

⅄

Hi Omnipotent Divine!
Do I see the glint in Your eyes
in steering Your humble creation for Your recreation

⅄

You are indeed the Playwright and the Director
I am the actor and entertainer in this play
What's the object of this never-ending world drama?

⅄

What is the purpose of life in this spectacular planet
End of the day, is life in this world a comedy or a tragedy?
In conclusion are we placed in this world with a return pass to another planet for another life?

⅄

ABOUT THE AUTHOR

The author of this book Errakiah Sannasi is a B.A (Hons) and Diploma-in-Education (1973) graduate of University Malaya. He began his career as a school teacher, served as a lecturer cum librarian in Teacher Training Institutes in Malaysia and retired in 2005 as Head of Library Science Department, IPBA.

In the year 2009 he implemented a nation-wide educational program called 'Newspaper-in-Education' for Tamil schools In Malaysia via a joint sponsorship program by a Tamil Daily-Makkal Osai and Dr. Rama Subbiah Scholarship Fund.

Quotations have been his passion. After his retirement from International Languages Teacher Training Institute K.Lumpur he penned his first book of poems-'Reflections of a Dreamer'. Wherein he focused on environmental and social adversities.

In this author's second text entitled Expressions of an Educator, the wisdom and humor in the Sayings are indeed remarkable. As a matter of fact this book is deemed to be worthy of its keep. It is indeed an invaluable piece of work to be preserved in libraries and homes. Work is Worship and Service is Prayer.

—R. Ganasa Murthi, Director IPBA 1999–2003

Kuala Lumpur, Malaysia

ACKNOWLEDGEMENTS

My profound appreciation to the following educationists and associates for sharing their viewpoints. Their appraisals indeed have enhanced the presentation of my Expressions in a precise and to the point manner:

Mdm. Au Sook Meng, MSc., exHead of Eng. Dept. IPBA -Chief Editor Mr. Suppiah Ramasamy, Msc., ex Head of Eng. Dept. MP Sandakan Miss. Priyanika Kiripananthan; Mr. Venkatagiri Balakrishnan Mr. Munusamy Jayaraman Naidu; Mr. Srinivaasan Rao Errakiah

A big thank you to Mdm. Soon Hong Chu who designed the cover and worked meticulously on the illustrations for the text.

My deepest appreciation to my friends and loved ones especially my wife V. K. Yogamalar for being my sturdy source of inspiration.

Without her encouragement and assistance certainly this product would not have been possible.

Special thanks to all readers, educationists, students, distributors, resource centers and academic institutions for their appraisals and reviews and for supporting my book.

"The greatest mystery in life is in not knowing
what is awaiting us next"

www.ingramcontent.com/pod-product-compliance
Lightning Source LLC
LaVergne TN
LVHW021142160826
845679LV00023B/2006

* 9 7 9 8 8 9 5 1 9 8 5 5 1 *